PROSPECT

C0-ASM-258

CORK & WOOD CRAFTS

CORK & WOOD CRAFTS

by Arden J. Newsome

illustrated by Nancy Coner

The Lion Press
New York

Dedicated to one matchless husband and three corkers—Mike, Donna, and Christopher.

Copyright © 1970 by Arden J. Newsome
Published by The Lion Press
52 Park Avenue, New York, N.Y. 10016   7702P
All rights reserved
Published simultaneously in Canada by George J. McLeod, Ltd.
73 Bathurst Street, Toronto 2B, Ontario
ISBN: 0-87460-228-9; Lib. ed: 0-87460-229-7
Library of Congress Catalog Card Number: 72-112370
This book was printed and bound in the United States of America

Contents

Introduction

This book is planned to give you hours of fun and to show you how you can make toys, decorations, gifts and many other projects from corks and pieces of wood that are easy to find around the house. If you decide to buy materials for some of the projects, such as cork sheets and balls, they will be inexpensive.

None of the projects is difficult. All you need is a little patience, imagination and a large grocery carton. In the carton, keep all your tools and materials: clothespins, toothpicks, popsicle sticks, bottle corks, soda bottle caps, cork ball fish floats, wooden berry baskets, etc. If it's made of cork or wood—start saving it! You will also need pencils, lightweight paper, scissors, a paper punch, glue, a ruler, and a knife with a serrated edge. (It has teeth, like a saw.) On page 63 you will find a list of materials and stores where you can buy them.

This book gives you only a few suggestions. Once you learn to work with the materials, use your imagination—you'll find you have dozens of new ideas. The more original your creations are, the more fun you can have! But before you choose your first project, be sure to read page 8.

Before You Begin

Whenever you begin a project, read the directions completely before you start, so that you will know what materials you will be using, and what steps to follow. As you work, read each instruction carefully, don't rush and always allow time for glued or painted parts to dry.

If a pattern or design is provided, place a piece of lightweight paper, such as tissue paper, over it. Trace the pattern with a pencil, and transfer it to your material with a piece of carbon paper, or by rubbing your pencil heavily over the back of your tracing first and then transferring it. Cutting patterns out of the book will ruin it for others.

Always be careful when you are working with a knife or a sharp, pointed tool. Keep your fingers away from the edge of the knife, and always cut away from your hands. Remember to protect the table or working surface from scratches and spills by using several layers of newspaper.

The materials you will need to make your cork and wood projects are described on page 63. Remember: for the best results, if you are working with adhesives, paints or plastic spray, always follow the instructions which appear on the can or package.

1. TOYS
1. TOYS
1. TOYS
1. TOYS
1. TOYS
1. TOYS
1. TOYS
1. TOYS
1. TOYS
1. TOYS
1. TOYS
1. TOYS
1. TOYS
1. TOYS
1. TOYS

Beagle Bowling Pins

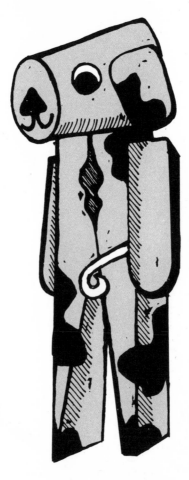

EAR PATTERN

Make this beagle with a clip clothespin and a bottle cork about 1″ long and ¾″ in diameter. The diameter is the width of a circle across its center.

Glue the cork head to the top of the clothespin body. Trace ear pattern and transfer to a cork sheet, ¹⁄₁₆″ thick. Cut out two ears. Glue in place. For arms, cut a wooden coffee stirrer in half. You can do this with scissors if they are sharp enough. Put one half away. Cut the remaining piece in half again. Bor-row an emery board from your mother. Sand the cut ends of the wood pieces with the emery board, rounding off the corners. Glue an arm to each side of body.

Using felt-tipped pens, paint eyes and a nose on the beagle's head and brown spots on his body. Now make nine more beagles, so you'll have ten pins. Find a small ball—cork or rubber—about 2″ in diameter. Set up the dog pins, and bowl 'em over!

Cork Kitten

To make this cork cat, you will need a cork ball 1″ in diameter for the head, a bottle cork 1¼″ long and 1″ in diameter for the body, some round toothpicks and a scrap of cork sheet, ¹⁄₁₆″ thick.

Cut toothpicks with scissors into correct lengths for the legs, tail and neck. Make legs about 1¼″ long, tail 1½″ long and neck about ¾″ long. Put the cat together by pushing toothpicks into the corks. If you have trouble pushing through the cork, make holes first with a large darning needle.

Trace the ears on the cork sheet. Cut them out, then glue them on the head. Hold the ears in place until the glue is dry. Paint a face with felt-tipped pens. Cut a straw—taken from your mother's broom—into four 1″ long pieces. Make holes in the cat's face with a darning needle, and push in the straw whiskers.

EAR PATTERN

The body of this airplane is made from a round clothespin. Trace the propeller and transfer it to the flat bottom of a disposable aluminum foil pan. (The kind of pan which comes with frozen food.) Cut out the propeller. Bend the two blades so that they tilt in opposite directions. Push a thumbtack into the propeller where the dot appears on the pattern. Now hammer the tack into the top of the clothespin, letting it extend up a bit so that the propeller spins freely.

Trace the wing and tail on a piece of cardboard. Cut out two pieces for each shape. Glue the two wings together. With the notch in the wings facing the front of the plane, slide the wings between the clothespin legs. Paste in place. Glue the tail together up to the tab line. Bend the tabs out, folding along the line. The tabs should face in opposite directions. Glue the bottom of the tabs in place on the top back of the body. Paint the plane any way you like.

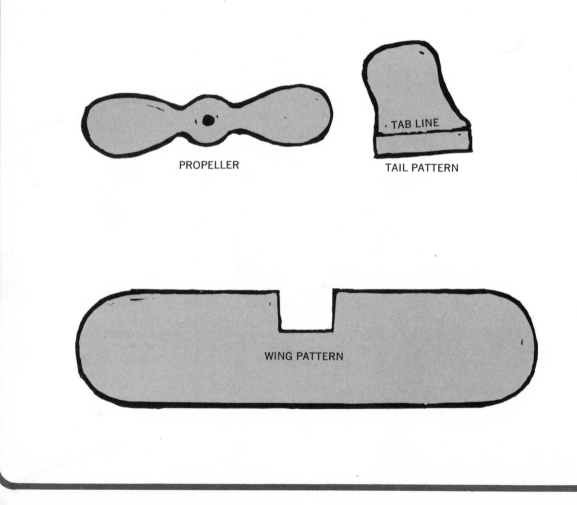

PROPELLER

TAB LINE

TAIL PATTERN

WING PATTERN

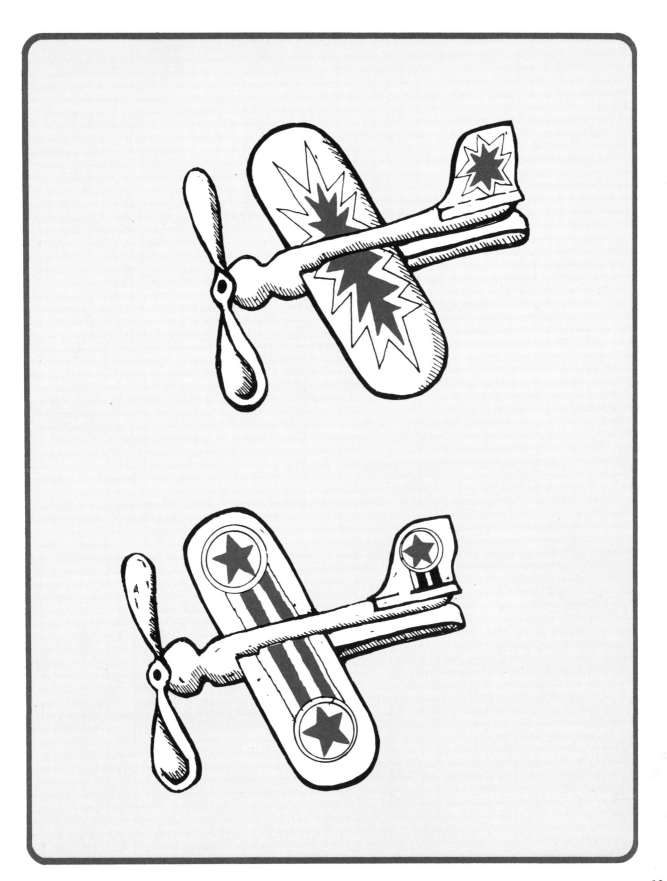

Paint a face on the back of a wooden picnic spoon. Use felt-tipped pens. Make an egg-shaped ball with absorbent cotton. Glue it into the bowl of the spoon (behind the face). Cut a few strands of knitting yarn into a small pile of tiny pieces. Put glue all over the cotton, and press the yarn pieces into the glue. Let them dry. Now brush off any loose pieces, and add more glue and yarn to the bare spots. Repeat until the doll's head is covered with yarn hair. Glue a little yarn around the face, too.

To make a puppet dress, fold a small handkerchief in half. Fold it in half again. Cut off a little part of the folded corner to make the neck of the dress. Cut the hole just large enough to fit the spoon handle.

Open the handkerchief. Fold it in half again. On one half, about 1″ down from neck hole, cut two more holes large enough to fit your thumb and forefinger. Make the holes 3″ apart and about 5½″ from the side edges, depending on the size of the hanky.

Slip the dress over the spoon handle. Hold the handle, under the dress, and put your thumb and forefinger out through the holes. Now your doll has arms. Say something. Your doll talks!

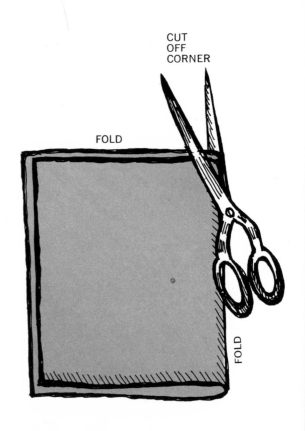

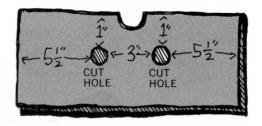

For Pinocchio's body, glue together the small ends of two corks 1¼″ high and 1″ in diameter. Trace the collar pattern and transfer it to a ¹⁄₁₆″ thick cork sheet. Cut out a small hole in the center.

Cut the burnt end off a matchstick. This will be the neck. Put glue on one end of the matchstick and push it into a 2″ cork ball. Make a hole in one end of the body, right in the center of the cork. Push the matchstick neck through the hole in the collar. Now glue the end of the matchstick in place on top of the body.

For legs, use two wooden candy apple sticks or two thin dowel sticks 4″ long. Make holes in the bottom of the body, and glue the legs into the holes. With a serrated knife, cut a cork, the same size used for the body, in half lengthwise. Make a hole in each half cork, on the curved side, back near the wide end. Now glue the legs in the cork feet.

For arms, break a popsicle stick in half. Use an emery board to sand the broken end until it is smooth and even. Paste an arm at each side of the body.

Find a tiny cork about ½″ high. Attach it to Pinocchio's head for a nose. Cut a few strands of knitting yarn into twelve 4″ pieces. Glue the yarn strands to the top of the head for hair. To make the hat, slice a ¼″ piece off the wide end of a 1¼″ bottle cork. Glue it to the wide end of a 1″ high cork.

Paint the hat and Pinocchio's face. Paint the collar, top body cork and sleeves to look like a jacket. Make the lower body cork a solid color for pants and paint the cork shoes black. Leave the cork head, neck, ends of arms and legs their natural color. Attach Pinocchio's hat with a short piece of toothpick pushed into the head.

COLLAR PATTERN

This ring toss game is fun to play alone. If a friend plays with you, the players compete for high score.

The figure's head will be a cork ball, 1″ in diameter. Glue it to the top of a clip clothespin. Make the base from a 4″ by 4″ square of scrap wood. If it is too thin, the base will fall over easily. It should be at least ½″ thick for balance. Now, glue the clothespin figure upright in the center of the wood square. Paint the base and figure, and don't forget to add a face and hair.

Trace the ring pattern on a sheet of cork, ⅛″ thick. Cut out three rings. Plain plastic bangle bracelets make good rings, too. Your mother or sister may have some they no longer want.

Make another ring toss figure and three more rings.

To play ring toss, place the figures about 4 feet or more apart. You stand next to one figure and your friend stands next to the other. Let your friend be first to toss his three rings at your figure. Then it's your turn. A ring over the figure counts 5 points. The first player who scores 25 points is the winner.

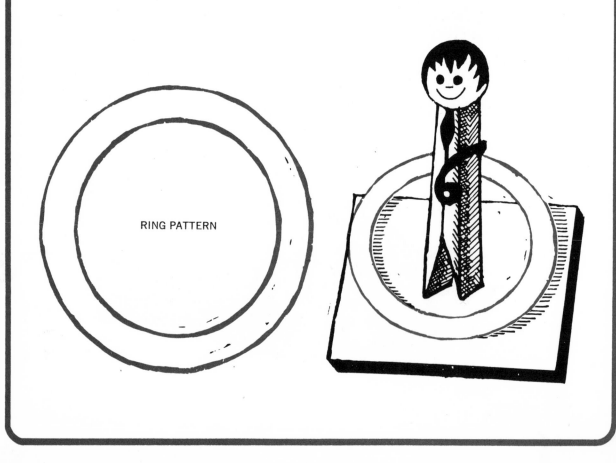

RING PATTERN

If your father or anyone you know makes things from wood, ask for the scraps from the discard pile. Collect a variety of shapes, sizes and thicknesses.

Take a look at the wood shapes. Does one of them resemble a fish or a bird? If you saw a piece off one of the shapes, will it look like a turtle? Use your imagination and a saw, if necessary, to make lots of scrappy creatures. Sand all the wood pieces smooth.

Paint your creatures in bright colors with detail lines and facial features in black. Use felt-tipped pens or poster paints. Spray the creatures with plastic spray when the paint is dry.

If any of your animals need ears or tails, cut them out of a ¹⁄₁₆″ cork sheet. Glue or thumbtack the cork pieces in place.

2. GIFTS AND THINGS

2. GIFTS AND THINGS
2. GIFTS AND THINGS
2. GIFTS AND THINGS
2. GIFTS AND THINGS
2. GIFTS AND THINGS
2. GIFTS AND THINGS
2. GIFTS AND THINGS
2. GIFTS AND THINGS
2. GIFTS AND THINGS
2. GIFTS AND THINGS
2. GIFTS AND THINGS
2. GIFTS AND THINGS
2. GIFTS AND THINGS
2. GIFTS AND THINGS

Trace the flower pattern on a $\frac{1}{16}''$ thick cork sheet. Cut it out. Glue the flower in the center of a flat wooden ice cream spoon. Glue a wooden button, 1″ in diameter, in the middle of the flower. Find four tiny beads, just a little larger than the holes for thread in the button. If your button has two holes, you'll need only two beads. Glue the beads in the holes.

Paint the flower your favorite color. The wooden spoon leaves are painted green. Let the paint dry thoroughly. Brush on a coat of clear nail polish. Attach a safety pin to the back of the flower with a piece of adhesive tape, and your pin is ready to wear.

FLOWER PATTERN

Cube Paperweight

This is a great desk accessory to make as a special gift. Use a 4″ by 4″ by 4″ cube of wood, smoothly sanded. Trace the pattern you like best and transfer it to a ¹⁄₁₆″ thick cork sheet. Cut it out. Glue the cork design to one side of the wood cube. Repeat this step six times until you have a design on every side of the cube.

Carefully paint only the cork pieces in the colors you prefer. Use felt marking pens or poster paints. Let the paint dry. Spray the whole block with clear plastic spray.

Mother would be thrilled with a flowered paperweight. And your father would be proud to have one with a boat design for his desk. Make up your own designs. Remember that the simpler the design is, the easier it will be to cut.

Flower Fob

This key chain fob is made of sheet cork with a wooden button center. Trace the flower pattern and transfer it to ⅛″ thick cork sheet. Cut out the shape. Glue a wooden button—about the size of the circle on the pattern—right in the middle of the flower.

Now trace the petal pattern on a cork sheet, 1/16″ thick. Cut out four petal shapes. Paint one side of each petal a flower color. Put glue on the unpainted backs and attach the petals to the flower.

Make a hole with an ice pick or a small paper punch near the edge of one petal. Give the flower a coat of clear nail polish. Insert a key chain through hole and your fob is complete. If you don't have a key chain, you can buy one at the dime store.

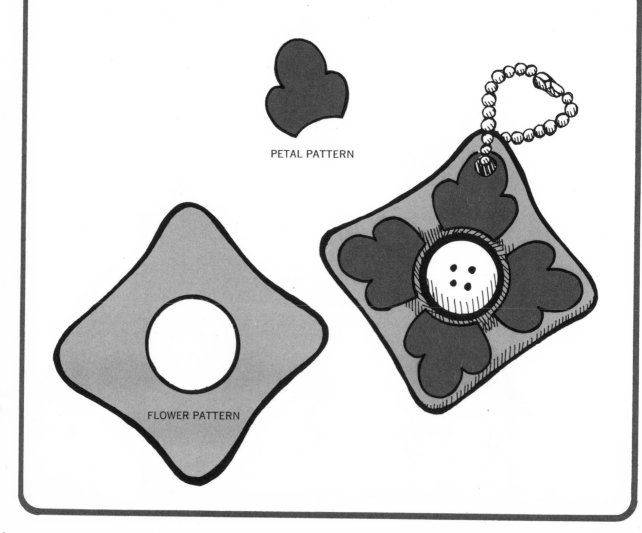

PETAL PATTERN

FLOWER PATTERN

Classy Clothespins

Mother will hang the prettiest wash in town with these clothespins. All you need is a package of wooden clip clothespins, felt-tipped pens and clear plastic spray.

Trace a design and transfer it to the flat sides of the clothespins. Color the design. When dry, spray with clear plastic spray. Make other designs using your own ideas. Draw them lightly on the clothespins with pencil before you paint.

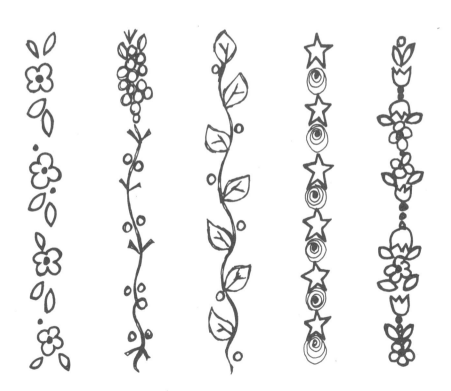

This lion bookmark is made from a bottle cork, 1¼″ high and 1″ in diameter, a ¹⁄₁₆″ thick cork sheet and yellow knitting yarn.

Transfer the mane pattern to the cork sheet. Cut out and glue it to the wide end of the bottle cork. With felt-tipped pens, paint a nose and a mouth on the cork end, eyes on the cork sides and ear markings on the mane. Don't forget: ears are at the top of the lion's head.

Bend a 2″ piece of flexible wire into a U-shape. Fold three 30″ long strands of yellow yarn in half, over the U-shaped wire. Twist the ends of the wire together once to hold the yarn. Place the wire under something heavy, like a large book, to hold the yarn securely while you braid it. You can also bend the wire around a doorknob or ask a friend to hold it as you braid the three strands. When you are 2″ from the end, tie the braid securely with another piece of yarn. With a darning needle, make 2 holes in the center back of the cork mane. Push the needle well into the cork head. Put glue on wire ends and push the wires all the way into the holes. The lion's tail will mark your place, while he looks out from the book you are reading.

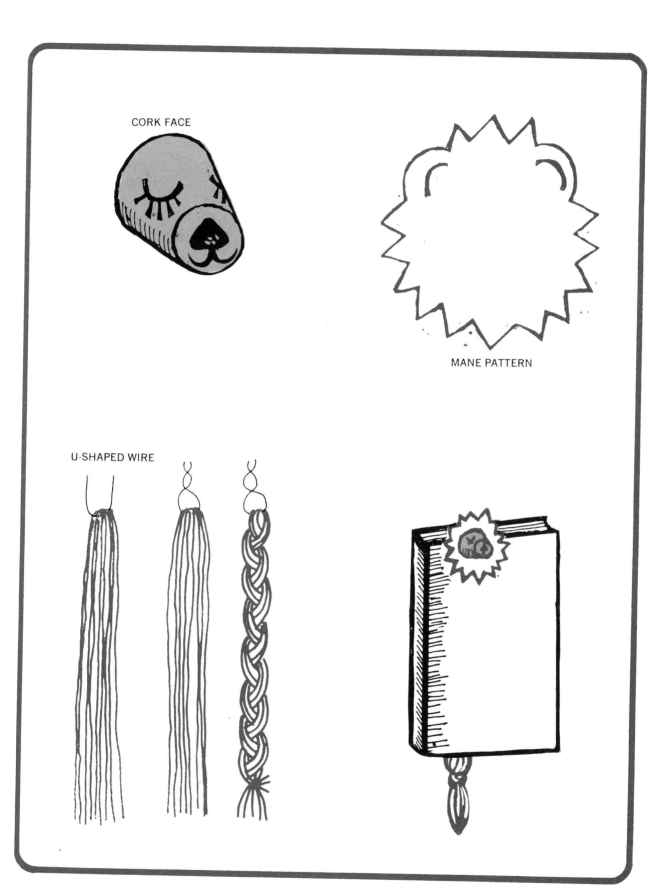

CORK FACE

MANE PATTERN

U-SHAPED WIRE

Matchstick Calendar

Your parents or friends will start the year off right with this gift. Begin by cutting a piece of corrugated cardboard 6¾″ long and 2½″ wide. Cut a piece of ¹⁄₁₆″ thick sheet cork the same size. Glue them together. The cork will be the front of the calendar. Make a frame by gluing burnt matchsticks all around the edge as shown. Cut matches with scissors to fit short ends.

Look through some used greeting cards or magazines for a picture to decorate the calendar. Cut out a picture about 1¾″ by 1¾″. Glue it in place on the cork, 1½″ from the top edge. Make a frame of burnt matchsticks around the picture.

Punch two holes near the top edge with an ice pick or paper punch. Spray the whole thing with clear plastic spray.

Paste a small calendar pad underneath the picture, near the bottom edge. You can buy a calendar pad at a stationery store. Through the holes, lace a ribbon, a shoelace or some fancy cord. Tie the ends in a bow in front, leaving a loop in the back for hanging the calendar.

If you wish, you can use a drawing or design of your own for a decoration. You might decide to paint the matchsticks instead of leaving them their natural color.

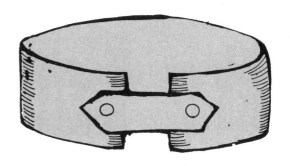

To make this cork bracelet you'll need a pattern. Make one from a strip of paper 1½″ wide and long enough to wrap tightly around your wrist (or arm if you wish to make an arm band). Use the paper pattern and cut the bracelet strip from the cork sheet, ⅛″ thick.

Paint one side of the cork strip with any design you wish, using felt-tipped markers. Punch a hole with an ice pick in each end of the strip, ½″ from the ends.

Cut a joining tab from the cork sheet, 1/16″ thick. Punch holes where shown on the pattern. Join tab to bracelet by matching holes and putting brass paper fasteners through both holes. Open the prongs on the inside of the bracelet.

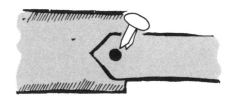

JOINING TAB
PATTERN

For each picture frame, trace, then transfer backing and frame pattern to $\frac{1}{16}''$ cork sheets. Cut them out. Color the design on the frame with felt-tipped pens.

Look among the snapshots taken of your family. Choose one for each member. Trim each snapshot to the same shape but just a little smaller than the backing pattern. Glue each photograph to the backing. Then paste the frame on top. (Be careful not to use too much glue.)

With a large darning needle, make a hole at the top and bottom of the frame, where the black dots are on the pattern. When you have framed each member of your family, make little joining rings from copper wire or pipe cleaners.

Wind wire once around a stick, about the size of a pencil, to form a ring. Cut wire with wire cutters or heavy scissors. Slip a ring in each frame hole and close it. Make another ring and join two frames together by linking this ring through the top ring of one frame and the bottom ring of the other. The last frame in the line will not need a bottom hole or ring.

Find a strip of wood about 6″ long, 1″ wide and about $\frac{1}{4}''$ thick. If you can't find a suitable wood strip, look to see if there's an old window shade around the house. The wood strip found in the bottom hem will be fine.

Have someone help you saw a piece 6″ long. Color a design on the wood like the one you painted on the frame. Spray the wood with clear plastic spray.

Put two small screw eyes in the top edge, about $\frac{1}{2}''$ from each end of the strip. Put another in the bottom edge, right in the middle of the strip.

Join the chain of frames by connecting the screw eye and the ring in the top frame with another wire ring. Tie a pretty piece of cord, or use a leather boot lace, to the top screw eyes as a hanging loop.

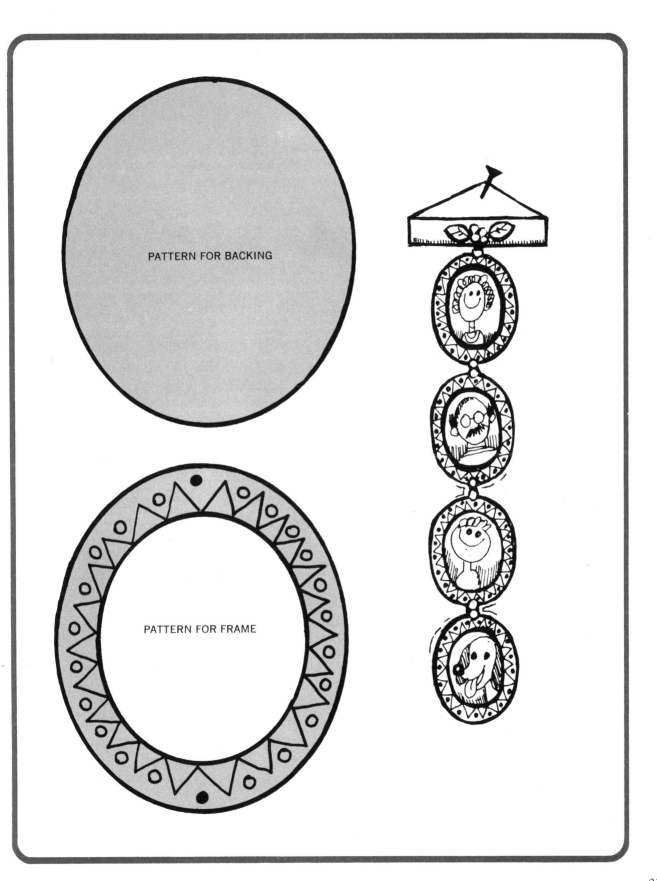

PATTERN FOR BACKING

PATTERN FOR FRAME

Collect some grasses, small flat flowers (such as violets and buttercups), wheat or rye heads, pretty weeds or whatever plant materials will look well grouped together in a picture. Put the plant material between 2 pieces of paper towel and press it until dry (about 2 weeks), under some heavy books.

From a cork sheet, ⅛″ thick, cut a plaque 10″ by 8″ or any size you wish. (If available, insulating cork can be used for plaques.) Arrange the plant material on the cork sheet. Move it around until you have an attractive picture.

Make a fence from a popsicle stick and 2 coffee stirrers. Break the popsicle stick in half for posts. Glue the coffee stirrers across the posts. Paint the fence, if you wish. Place the fence on the plaque.

Use a piece of dried bark and short branches of tiny leaves to make a tree. A slice of cork cut from the round end of a large bottle cork can be painted to look like an owl. Place the owl on a twig branch.

When you are pleased with the way the picture looks, glue the fence, owl and all the plant material in place with white glue. Add some tiny pebbles.

Use household glue and a thumbtack to attach a pull tab from a soda can to the back of the plaque as a hanger.

Jewelry Caddy

Ask for a paint mixing paddle at a paint store. They are usually free. Have an adult drill a hole for hanging in the handle. Paint the stick a solid color with poster paints and let it dry.

Paint four big flowers, evenly spaced, down the center of the stick. Screw an L-shaped curtain hook in the center of each flower. Spray the stick with clear plastic spray. Hang it on the wall in your room. It will keep your necklaces and chain belts from tangling.

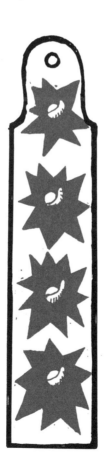

Picture Frame Bulletin Board

Find a large old picture frame. If it has glass, a picture and cardboard backing, remove them. Save the cardboard. Paint the frame a bright color. Let it dry. Spray with clear plastic spray.

Using the cardboard piece as a pattern, cut a piece the same size from a cork sheet $1/8''$ thick. Paint a design in one corner of the cork. Create a design of your own or trace the design shown.

Spread glue along the inside edges of the frame. Press the cork sheet inside the frame. Paste the cardboard to the back of the cork. Add a brass picture ring to the top of the frame. Hang up the bulletin board. Tack on your favorite pictures or notes reminding you of important dates.

Tricky Trivet

Trivets protect table tops from the heat of hot pots and pans. To make this trivet you will need a smoothly sanded square of wood, 6″ by 6″ and ¼″ thick, two 5″ by 5″ squares of cork sheet, ⅛″ thick, some colored thumb tacks and a tack hammer.

Spray the wood piece with 2 light coats of clear plastic spray. When dry, glue one of the cork squares to the wood square. (This will be the bottom.) Center the cork so that an equal amount of wood shows all around the edges. Put a heavy book on the cork until the glue is dry.

Cut a scalloped border, like the one shown, all around the edge of the other cork square. Place the cork on the top of the wood piece. Center it. Attach cork to wood by hammering a tack through the cork and into the wood at every scallop.

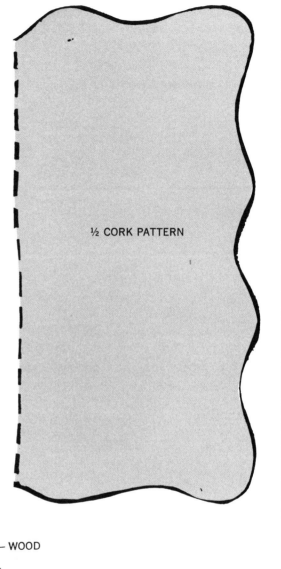

½ CORK PATTERN

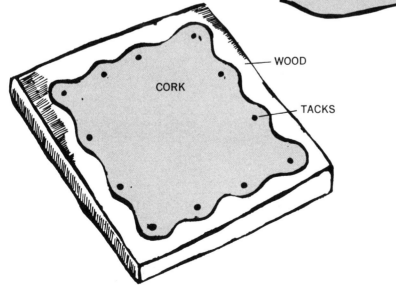

WOOD

CORK

TACKS

To make this funny, twisting mobile, use one section of a 6″ wide wooden embroidery hoop, a cork sheet, $\frac{1}{16}$″ thick, strong black carpet thread and a sewing needle.

Trace the patterns and transfer them to the cork sheet. Cut them out. Be sure to cut the correct number of hands, feet, ears and eyes. Paint all the cork pieces and the embroidery hoop head with poster paints.

Thread the needle with a long piece of thread. Knot one end. Push the needle through the center of the mouth as indicated by a dot on the pattern. Tie the thread to the inside of the embroidery hoop. Let the mouth hang on a 5″ thread. Cut off excess thread.

Attach eyes to the embroidery hoop in the same way with 2″ lengths of thread. The eyes tie at each side of the mouth thread. Glue the ears at each side of the head putting them on the back edge of the hoop.

Tie the body pieces to the hoop. Attach the shirt with a 1″ length of thread. Then join pants to shirt, also with a 1″ thread. Feet dangle from pants' legs with 1½″ threads and the hands are attached to the shirt shoulders with 3″ thread lengths.

Cut about ten 6″ lengths of yarn to use as hair. Tie the center of the yarn strands to the top center of the hoop head with one end of the long part of a hanging thread. Hang the other end of the thread from a nail in a windy spot and watch the mobile dance.

You can make larger or smaller mobile men by adjusting the patterns and lengths of thread and by using smaller or larger embroidery hoops.

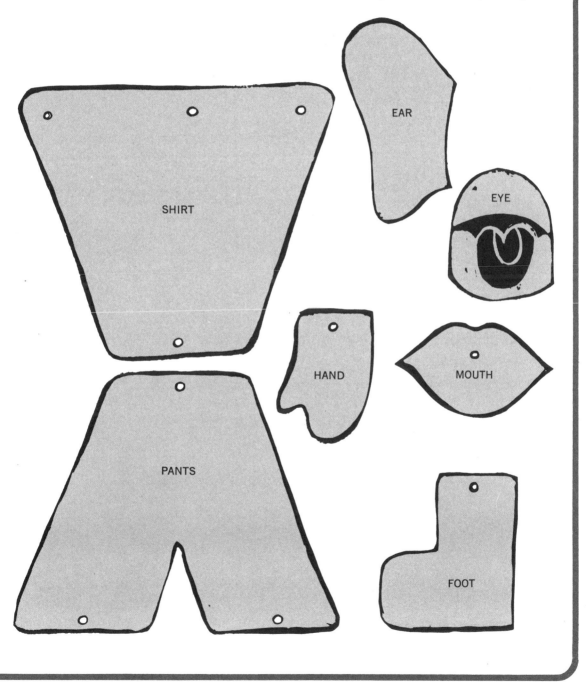

To make this trinket box, use a large kitchen matchbox and wood from berry baskets. Wooden berry baskets are made of very thin wood. They break and cut easily.

First remove the inside drawer from the matchbox. Paint the drawer white, inside and out. Now paint the outside box white. Let it dry and give it a coat of clear plastic spray.

Cut berry basket wood into small pieces. Make squares, rectangles, strips and triangles. Cover the box with the wood mosaic pieces. Leave enough space between each piece so that the white color shows through. Wipe off any excess glue which squeezes out from under the wood.

Cut two rectangular pieces of cork sheet, $\frac{1}{16}''$ thick, large enough to cover the ends of the inside drawer. Glue the cork in place. For a drawer knob, glue a large wooden bead to one end. Spray the inside drawer and outside box with plastic spray. Slide the drawer into the box, and it's ready to hold your special small treasures.

If you want to make a chest of drawers, just nest four or six finished drawers and glue them together—sides, top and bottom. Cut a cardboard or cork mat to fit the bottom and attach it with glue. It will hold the drawers together securely. Add a cork or cardboard top, too, if you like, and paint it or decorate it with pieces of wood. Almost any color looks nice with natural wood, so be as imaginative as you like when you paint the matchboxes.

Pot Holder Rack

Following the illustration, arrange the flowers and flower pots on the board. The bottle cork halves are the pots. The ball halves are flower centers. Place the two flowers so that they are spaced the same distance from the edges of the board. Glue all the pieces in place.

Screw a brass picture ring in the top edge of the board at the center. Screw two cup hooks in the bottom edge. Place them directly under the flowerpots. Spray the rack with clear plastic spray. Give it to your mother for Mother's Day!

HALF CORK

LOLLIPOP STICK

HALF CORK

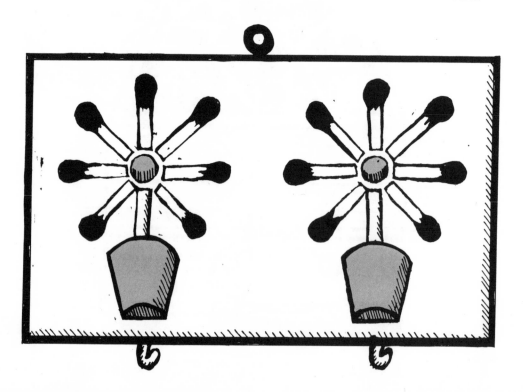

A set of these glass coasters would make a nice gift for almost anyone. They will protect furniture from wet glasses.

Find some jar lids all the same size, if you are making a set. They should be about 3″ in diameter and ½″ high. Paint the outside and bottom of each lid. If the poster paint does not stick to the metal lids, mix a little liquid soap in the paint. Let dry.

Turn the lids upside down and spray with a light coat of plastic spray. Then trim the outside of the coasters with rickrack or pretty braid.

Cut a circle of ⅛″ thick cork to fit inside each lid. Glue the cork circles in place. Turn the coasters upside down again and spray with clear plastic spray. Don't spray the cork inside the coaster, or it will not absorb moisture.

Make your dog or somebody's dog a gift. Find a nicely sanded piece of wood about 10″ long, 4″ wide and ½″ thick.

Trace the dog and ear patterns and transfer them to a ¹⁄₁₆″ thick cork sheet. Cut them out. Glue the cork dog to the board. Attach the ear, putting glue only on the top half.

Paint the board, and the dog's face and spots, with poster paint. When the paint is dry, screw a brass picture ring in the top edge of the board at the center. Where the dots appear on the pattern, screw three cup hooks into the board. Spray the caddy with clear plastic spray. Hang it up. The caddy is perfect for hanging your pet's collar and leash, brush and towel.

EAR PATTERN

3. PARTY PROPS

3. PARTY PROPS
3. PARTY PROPS
3. PARTY PROPS
3. PARTY PROPS
3. PARTY PROPS
3. PARTY PROPS
3. PARTY PROPS
3. PARTY PROPS
3. PARTY PROPS
3. PARTY PROPS
3. PARTY PROPS
3. PARTY PROPS
3. PARTY PROPS
3. PARTY PROPS
3. PARTY PROPS

Military Favorite

To make this soldier party favor, glue a 1″ cork ball head to the top of a round clothespin. The clothespin should have a flat top.

Trace the arm and hat brim patterns and transfer them to a ¹⁄₁₆″ thick cork sheet. Cut out the brim and two arms. Glue the arms in place. To make the hat, glue the small end of a 1″ high cork to the hat brim.

Paint the soldier with poster paints. Make head and hands a skin color, the top part of the clothespin, arms and hat red. Paint the bottom of the clothespin blue, making the very ends black for shoes. Let dry.

Then paint on your soldier's face, hair, and a blue hat band. Glue two sequins on the hat and front of the jacket. Attach the hat to the soldier's head with a short piece of toothpick pushed into both pieces. Tie metallic gift-wrapping cord around the body as shown.

To make a stand, glue the soldier to a 2″ by 2″ square of thin wood or corrugated cardboard. Paint the stand. Stick a piece of tape—magic mending or adhesive—on the stand. Write your party guest's name on the tape.

ARM PATTERN

BRIM PATTERN

Use a 1″ high bottle cork, 1¼″ in diameter, for this flower pot. Take three round toothpicks and break off a small end from two of them. This will make stems of three different lengths. Push the stems into the large end of the cork.

Find 3 small beads and 3 tiny beads. Wooden ones are nice, but you can use any beads that have holes large enough to fit the toothpicks. Glue the bead flowers in place at the top of the stems as shown. Cut four leaves from scraps of cork sheet, 1/16″ thick. Glue them to stems as shown.

Paint pot, leaves, and posies. Let dry. For a nice shiny finish, paint again with clear nail polish.

Put the pot in the center of a 4″ square of aluminum foil. Mold foil up around the pot, like a real gift plant. Tie a narrow ribbon bow around the foil. Party guests will enjoy taking this favor home.

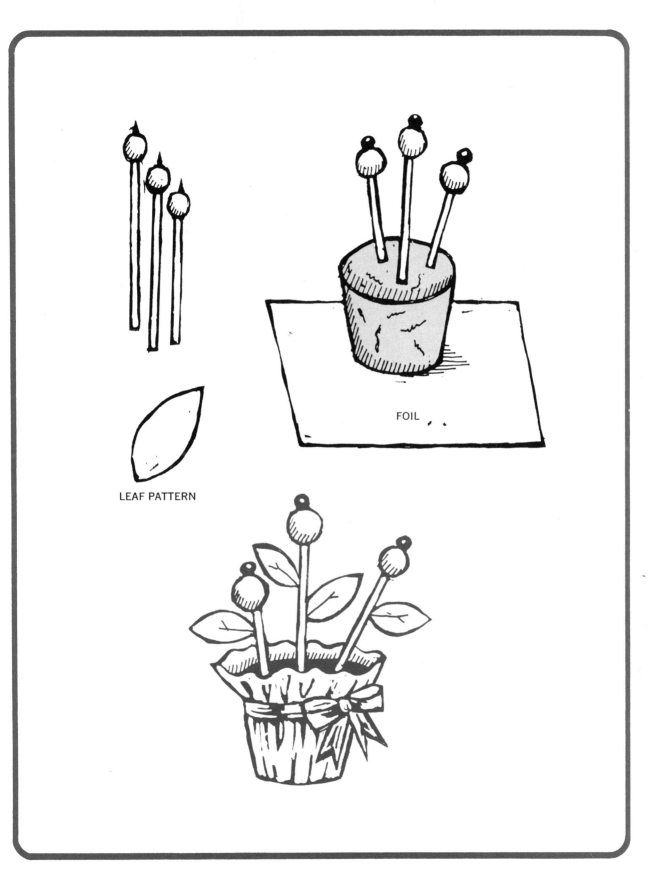

LEAF PATTERN

FOIL

To make these unusual dolls, first remove the spring from a clip clothespin. Just give the wood pieces a twist in opposite directions and they will come apart easily. Glue the two flat sides of the wood together.

For arms, cut two pieces from a wooden coffee stirrer, each about 1¼″ long. With sharp scissors, you can cut the stirrer easily. With an emery board, sand and round off the ends. Glue arms in place.

Make a stand for the figure from a piece of thin wood or corrugated cardboard, 2″ by 2″. Spread glue on the bottom of legs and attach the doll to the stand. Color doll and stand with poster paints or felt-tipped pens. Paint her hair, face, dress and shoes.

PENNANT

Following the pattern, cut out a pennant of white paper. Write your guest's name on the pennant and glue it to a flat toothpick. Tape or glue it in the doll's hand.

A Christmas angel is made in the same way, but glue ice cream spoon wings to the back of her body before painting. If the spoon you have is not shaped exactly like the one shown or has two different ends, shape with an emery board until both ends look the same.

Spooky Sipper

This Hallowe'en pumpkin straw begins with a 1½″ wide cork ball. Make a hole through the ball the same width as a thin drinking straw.

Paint the ball orange, using poster paints. When dry, paint on black eyes, nose and a toothy grin.

For the hat, trace the patterns and cut them from black construction paper. Punch a hole in the center of the brim. Overlap the straight edges of the crown and glue them together. Cut a little part off the crown point to make a hole the size of the straw.

Glue the crown in the center of the hat brim. Glue the hat on top of the pumpkin's head. Be sure the hole in the hat brim is over the hole in the pumpkin's head. Spray the pumpkin with clear plastic spray.

Push a straw through the pumpkin until it extends several inches out of the top of the hat. To keep this spooky sipper in place on the straw, tie a green ribbon right under the pumpkin's chin. Tie it loosely or you won't be able to sip your Hallowe'en cider.

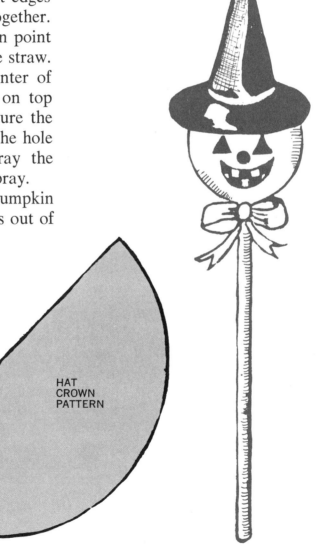

CUT
OUT
HOLE

BRIM PATTERN

HAT
CROWN
PATTERN

This game should be prepared before your birthday party starts. Get a wooden ice cream spoon and a birthday candle for each guest.

With a black felt-tipped pen write one guest's name on each spoon. Paint a black line around the end of each candle. Be sure the line is in the same place on each candle. With a drop or two of melted wax, attach a candle to the center of each spoon boat. (Let an adult help you.) During the party fill a large shallow bowl, pan or tub (depending on how many guests you have at your party) with water. Place all boats in the water. Ask the adults to light the candles so that each candle has an equal chance to win.

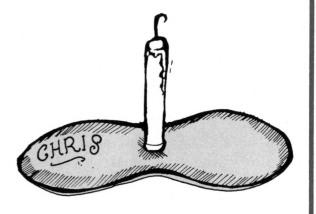

The guest whose candle burns down to the black line first wins a prize.

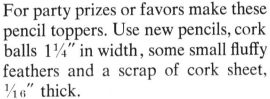

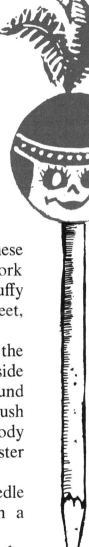

For party prizes or favors make these pencil toppers. Use new pencils, cork balls 1¼″ in width, some small fluffy feathers and a scrap of cork sheet, ¹⁄₁₆″ thick.

Cut the wings for the bird from the cork sheet. Glue a wing to each side of the ball body. Break the round ends off 2 flat toothpicks and push them into the front of the ball body for a beak. Paint the bird with poster paints. When dry, paint on eyes.

Make a hole with a darning needle in the back of the body. Push a feather into the hole for a tail.

To make the Indian, paint the hair, headband and mouth on a cork ball. Use black thumbtacks for eyes. Push 2 feathers into the top of the ball head.

Maypole Centerpiece

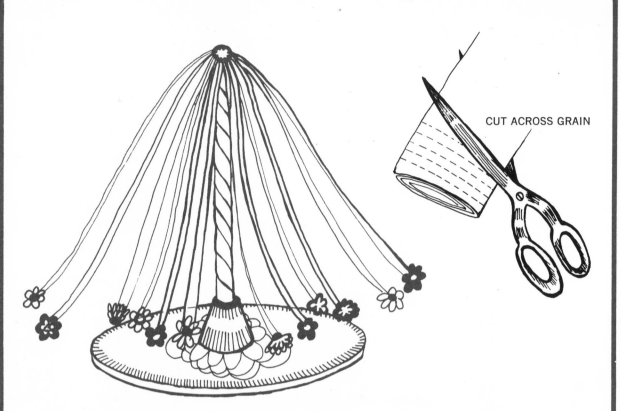

CUT ACROSS GRAIN

Celebrate May Day with a centerpiece made from a new pencil with an eraser, a 3″ wide cork circle, ⅛″ thick (cork circles may be purchased at craft shops, or you can cut one from a cork sheet), a bottle cork about 1″ high and 1¼″ wide, white crepe paper, a thumbtack and some old flowered greeting cards.

Glue the wide end of the bottle cork in the center of the cork circle.

Next, cover the pencil Maypole. Cut a 14″ long strip of crepe paper, about ½″ wide. Sharpen the pencil to a blunt point. Take the end of the crepe paper and, starting at the top near the eraser, wrap the paper spirally around the pencil down to where the sharpened part begins. A small amount of glue will hold the crepe paper in place.

Make a hole in the top end of the cork stand with an ice pick. Push the pointed end of the pencil into the hole until all of the sharpened point is hidden.

Cut 5 strips of crepe paper, all about 12″ long. Glue a small flower cut from a greeting card to the end of each strip. Glue some flowers around the cork stand.

Take the center of each paper strip and lay it across the top of the pencil eraser. Push thumbtack into eraser to hold the Maypole streamers in place.

4. HAPPY HOLIDAYS
4. HAPPY HOLIDAYS
4. HAPPY HOLIDAYS
4. HAPPY HOLIDAYS
4. HAPPY HOLIDAYS
4. HAPPY HOLIDAYS
4. HAPPY HOLIDAYS
4. HAPPY HOLIDAYS
4. HAPPY HOLIDAYS
4. HAPPY HOLIDAYS
4. HAPPY HOLIDAYS
4. HAPPY HOLIDAYS
4. HAPPY HOLIDAYS
4. HAPPY HOLIDAYS
4. HAPPY HOLIDAYS
4. HAPPY HOLIDAYS
4. HAPPY HOLIDAYS

Make this Christmas card for a special friend. Don't mail it; deliver it when you visit. The card is special because it can be hung on a Christmas tree.

Using the pattern, cut one house from ⅛″ thick cork and one from white construction paper. From ¹⁄₁₆″ thick cork, cut a window and a door, both 1½″ by 1″. Glue them in place on the house as shown. With felt-tipped pens, paint lines on the window, a wreath on the door and a green Christmas tree on the house.

Write "Merry Christmas from our house to your house," or any other message you like, on the white paper shape. Glue it to the back of the cork house. On the front, paste a sequin on the door for a knob. Frame the house with flat toothpicks. Glue one at each side first, then put one on each side of roof.

Put tiny dots of glue on the Christmas tree. Sprinkle on white glitter snow while the glue is wet. Finally, punch a hole with an ice pick at the top of the house. Add a red ribbon loop for hanging. Find the right size envelope, and put your card inside. If you wish, decorate the envelope with felt-tipped markers.

FRONT

BACK

Merry Christmas from our House to yours

55

With an ice pick or a nail make a hole lengthwise through four small corks, about 1″ high. Paint the corks green, using poster paints. Brush each cork with clear nail polish.

Tie one end of a 10″ length of red knitting yarn to a small jingle bell. Thread the other end into a large darning needle. Push the needle through a cork from the wide end. Pull it and the yarn out the top. Remove the needle. Attach bells to the other three corks in the same way.

Hold all the yarn strands together. Tie a knot in the yarn, about 1″ above the corks. Tie the yarn above the knot into a bow. Attach this bell pin to your coat with a small safety pin, or use it to decorate a special package.

STEP 1.

STEP 2.

STEP 3.

Curtain Ring Wreath

Wooden curtain rings can be turned into pretty tree decorations. Paint the ring green. Spray with plastic spray. Using glue, attach tiny red sequins in groups of three around the ring for berries. Take some narrow ribbon and make a tiny bow. Glue this to the top of the wreath, just in front of the eye.

With another piece of ribbon, make a loop through the eye.

Hang the wreath on your Christmas tree. If you'd like to use the wreath as jewelry, omit the ribbon loop. Put a necklace chain through the eye and wear the wreath around your neck!

Wooden coffee stirrers are used to make this unique decoration. Hang several trees in a window, from the ceiling, or even on your Christmas tree.

Glue three coffee stirrers together to form a triangle. Attach two more stirrers, placing them diagonally across the tree shape. Cut them to size with scissors.

Turn the tree over. Glue two more stirrers diagonally across the tree, crisscrossing the other diagonal sticks. Cut two 1¾″ pieces of stirrer. Glue them to the center of the bottom stick for a trunk.

Paint the tree and trim it with sequins or glitter. Tie a thread loop at the top of your tree for hanging.

STEP 1.　　　　STEP 2.　　　　STEP 3.

To make these toothpick and shiny paper ornaments, start by tracing the different pattern shapes. Transfer the shapes to metallic gift wrap paper —the kind which is foil on one side and paper on the other.

Cut out two pieces for each shape. Spread glue on the paper side of one shape. Press round colored toothpicks on top, making all the pick ends meet in the center of the shape. Spread glue on the paper back of another identical shape. Lay it on top of the toothpicks and press the two shapes together.

You can cut some toothpicks in half so your design will have long and short points. You can lay toothpicks on the shape in any design you wish. Now, using glue, attach sequins to the tips of each toothpick.

Last, thread a needle with silver, gold or green thread. Push the needle through one edge of the paper shape and make a thread loop. After you make these designs, try some of your own ideas.

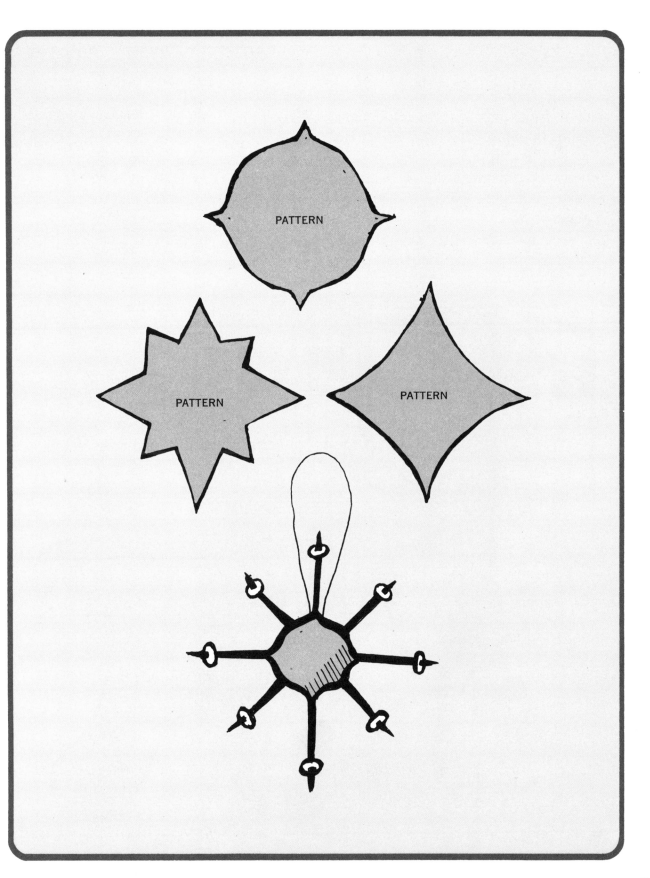

PATTERN

PATTERN

PATTERN

Using the pattern, cut a gingerbread man from a ⅛″ thick cork sheet. Paint on white "frosting" like a real cookie has. Spread glue all over the back of the gingerbread man and paste him to white construction paper.

Cut out the paper in the same shape. Punch a hole in the top of the head with a nail or ice pick. Write "To . . . From . . ." or whatever message you wish on the paper side. Glue a sequin face and buttons to the front. Add gold or silver gift-wrapping cord, and tie the cork cookie tag on a special gift. Tell the receiver he can hang the cookie on his Christmas tree.

PATTERN
FOR
GINGERBREAD
MAN

TO:
FROM:

List of Materials

CORK: Bottle and thermos corks come in many sizes. They can be purchased at any dime store. Cork balls and sheets can be bought at craft shops. Two 12″ by 36″ sheets, one each of ¹⁄₁₆″ and ⅛″ thickness, will go a long way. Save all scraps; the smallest piece can be used in some way. Cut cork sheets with scissors or an x-acto knife. Make holes in the ¹⁄₁₆″ thick sheet with a paper punch; use an ice pick or a nail for sheets ⅛″ thick. Bottle corks and balls are cut with the serrated knife, using a sawing motion. Cork balls usually come with holes. However, when holes must be put in bottle corks or balls, use an ice pick, a long nail, a thin knitting needle, or another similar tool. Tap the pick or nail with a small hammer, if you have difficulty pushing it through the cork.

WOOD: Use scrap pieces of soft woods such as pine and basswood. These are easy to work with. Coffee stirrers can be cut with scissors. Popsicle sticks can be broken or cut with an x-acto knife. If you find that pieces of scrap wood must be cut, use a coping saw and ask an adult to help you.

COLORS: Poster paints, felt-tipped pens and even crayons are fine to use. Sometimes the directions will tell you to finish the project with a coat of clear plastic spray paint or clear nail polish to give the project a protective finish. Whenever you use the plastic spray, first put your project in a large cardboard box, then ask an adult for help.

ADHESIVES: White liquid glue, such as Sobo, is excellent for cork, wood, paper, or any project in this book. It is transparent when dry, dries rapidly, and really holds things together. Paper paste is not satisfactory.

745.51
N

PROSPECT
7702

Newsome, Arden J
Cork & wood crafts

Date Due

	14'74		

Instructions for making a variety of objects from wood and cork.